I'm Reading About

TEXAS

The Lone Star State!

GALLOPADE

by Carole Marsh

Printed and Manufactured in Peachtree City, GA., USA
www.gallopade.com

Book design: John Hanson

Editorial manager: Janice Baker

Texas is a great state.

It is one of a kind.

What makes Texas special?

Let's read about it

and see!

NATIVE AMERICANS

Who lived in Texas first?

Native Americans did!

They moved around to find food.
They hunted in Texas' woods.
They fished in Texas' rivers.
They gathered fruits and seeds and nuts.

EXPLORERS

Spanish explorers came to Texas in 1541.

Francisco Vásquez de Coronado was their leader. He and his men were looking for cities of gold!

N
NE
E
SE
S
SW
W
NW

SETTLEMENT

Missionaries came to Texas to spread their religion.
They built the first mission at Ysleta.
It was near today's city of El Paso.

A mission was a place built to bring the Christian religion to the native people.

Mission

STATEHOOD

Texas was the 28th state
to join the United States of America!

Isn't it great,
to be a state!
I bet Texas
could hardly wait!

Texas became a state in 1845.

Texas
The 28th State
Here we are!

FLAG

I am the state flag.
I was adopted in 1839.

What colors am I?
Red. White. Blue.

Look at me.
What else do you see?
I have one white star!

I fly high over the state of Texas!

CAPITAL

Say hello to Austin:
the capital city of Texas!

There is an important building in Austin.
It is the State Capitol.
Texas laws are made there!

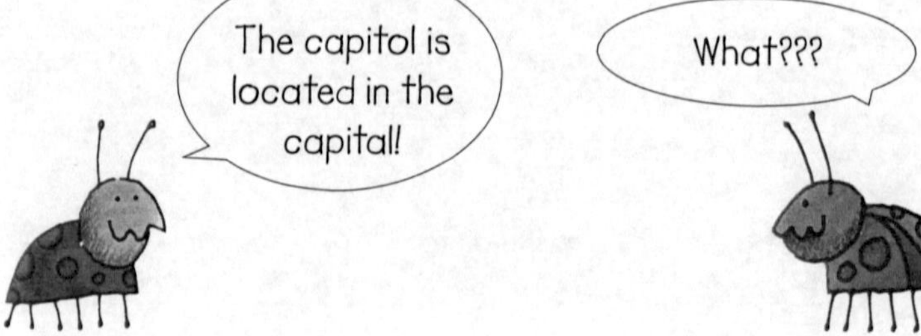

Capitol

Capital

SEAL

I am a seal,
but I am not the State Seal.
If I were, I would be very important.
I would be stamped on many official papers.
(Ouch, that might hurt!)

THE STATE OF TEXAS
Now, that's official!

NICKNAME

State nicknames are fun!
State nicknames are great!
They share fun facts
about each state!

Texas' nickname is "The Lone Star State."

Texas was an independent country for ten years.
The lone star reminds us of that!

The Lone Star State

BORDERS

Look at Texas.
Texas is in a region called "the Southwest."

Texas borders four other states.
It also borders the country of Mexico.
Find Texas and its neighbors on the map!

Borders

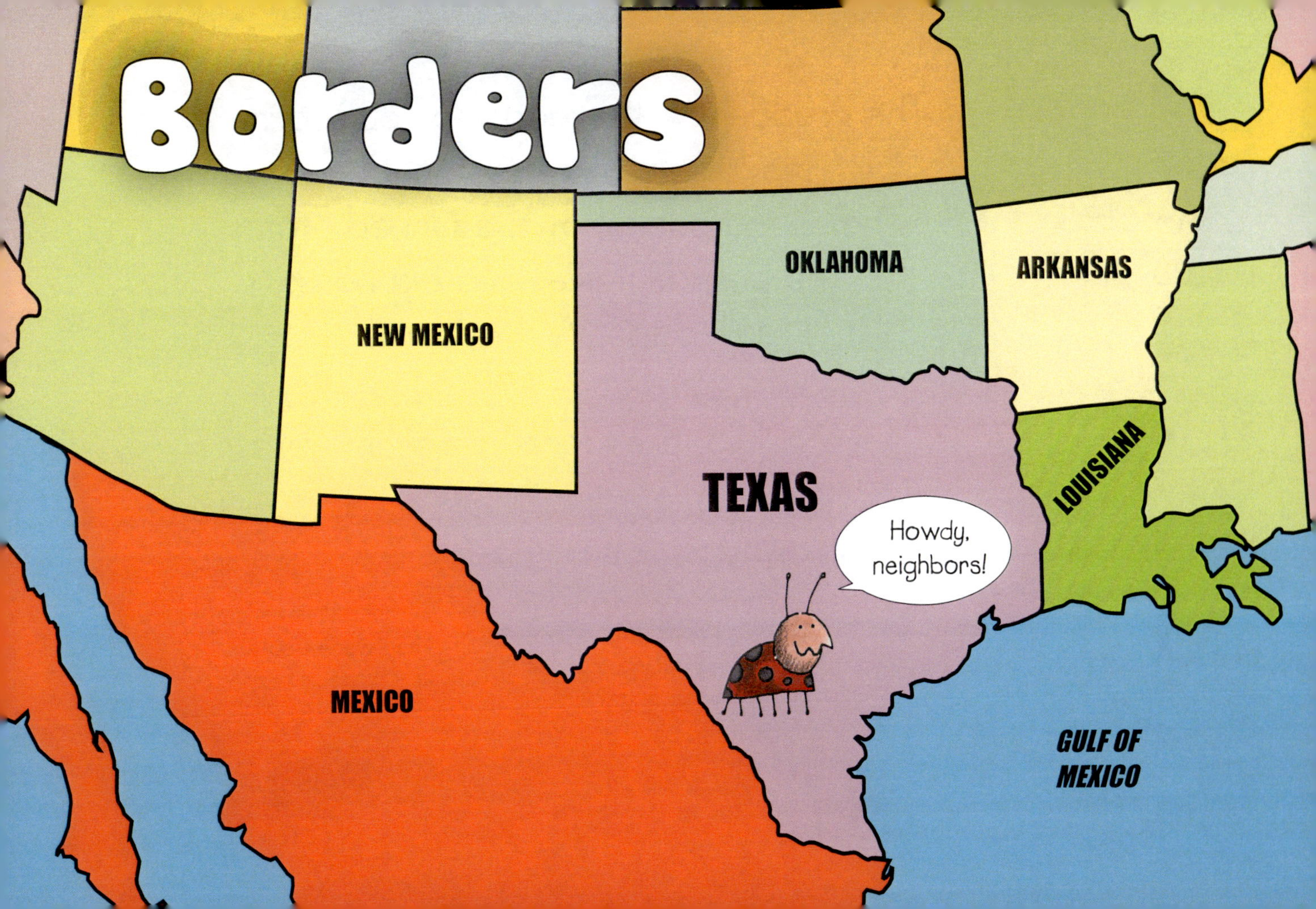
NEW MEXICO
OKLAHOMA
ARKANSAS
TEXAS
LOUISIANA
Howdy, neighbors!
MEXICO
GULF OF MEXICO

PRESIDENTS

The president is the leader of our country.
He lives in Washington, D.C.
That is the capital of the United States.
The president lives in a big house
called the White House.

Several U.S. presidents are from Texas!

Dwight Eisenhower
34th President
Lyndon Johnson
36th President
George H.W. Bush
41st President
George W. Bush
43rd President

PEOPLE

Many famous people

Stephen F. Austin
Father of Texas

Sam Houston
President of the Republic of Texas

Michael DeBakey
Pioneer in heart surgery

call our state home!

Mary Kay Ash
Founder of Mary Kay Cosmetics, Inc.

Barbara Jordan
First African American woman from the South to serve in the U.S. Congress

Nolan Ryan
Major League Baseball pitcher who set the record for most no-hitters

Mockingbird

I am the state bird, and I fly
over Texas, proud and high.

As I fly, up in the sky,
I flap my wings to tell you "Hi!"

The Texas state bird is the Mockingbird.

BIRD

Bluebonnet

FLOWER

I am the Bluebonnet.
I am the state flower.

I grow where it's warm and sunny.
I bloom in the spring.
I help make Texas beautiful!

Look at me! Smell me!
When I bloom, I turn fields into
blankets of blue!

Pecan Tree

TREE

I am a Pecan—I'm the state tree.
All over Texas you can find me.

The nuts I make are good to eat.
Pecans are always a tasty treat!

I stand up straight, big and tall.
Don't climb too high—it would hurt to fall!

Monarch Butterfly

INSECT

I am a Monarch Butterfly.
I am the state insect.

I flit and fly from flower to flower.
I am looking for nectar to drink.

Look at my beautiful wings.
What colors do you see?

Gulf of Mexico

BEACHES

Let's go to the beach!

We can swim in the waves.
We can play in the sand.

We can build a big castle
where water meets land.

Texas beaches are home to many animals:

Sea Turtles **Birds** **Crabs** **Dolphins** **and More!**

Guadalupe Peak

MOUNTAINS

The mountains in west Texas
are the place to be.
Hiking and camping
are fun for you and me.

Take lots of water for your mountain trip.
You will need more than just a sip!

Rio Grande

RIVER

The Rio Grande is one of the longest rivers in North America!
It is in southwest Texas.

The river habitat is home to many animals:

Birds **Deer** **Snakes** **Frogs** **Bats** **and More!**

The Rio Grande forms the border between the United States and Mexico!

The Alamo
Remember...
...the Alamo!

LANDMARK

The Alamo is an old mission church.
It is in San Antonio.
An important battle took place there in 1836.
Texas was fighting to be free from Mexico's rule!

The Texans lost the Battle of the Alamo.
But not long after the battle, they won the war!

Texas Crops

cotton

corn

wheat

Nursery Plants

Flowers are my personal favorite!

AGRICULTURE

Texas has many farms.
Why?
Because Texas has good soil and a warm climate!

Some of the top crops grown in Texas are:

Cotton **Corn** **Wheat** **Nursery Plants**

Hey!
Don't forget about me!
I am a Texas Longhorn.
My state is #1 in cattle production.
Yee ha!

Sports in Texas

SPORTS

Baseball! Basketball! Football!
Texas has it all.

Whether you like to watch or play,
You are sure to have a ball!

Astros **Rangers** **Mavericks**

Rockets **Spurs** **Cowboys**

Texans **Longhorns**

Aggies **& More!**

Texas: Home of the Oil Industry

Texas produces more oil than any other state!
Oil is very important.
It is used to make gasoline and many other products.

Nicknames for oil are
"Black Gold" and "Texas Tea."

GLOSSARY

climate: weather conditions in an area over a long period of time

elect: to choose someone by voting

gasoline: fuel used by cars and other vehicles

habitat: a place where plants or animals naturally live

independent: not being ruled by another country

laws: rules made by the government

nectar: a sweet liquid produced by plants, especially flowers

pioneer: the first to do something

region: an area that has similar characteristics

settlement: the first community in an area